inhospitably on your left, a mountain which Coleridge might have described as a 'Giant's Tent'. If you are lucky you might see a peregrine swoop from the bare rocks above. People once saw such mountains as dangerous, ugly places which should be avoided. Daniel Defoe described them as 'barren and wild, of no use or advantage either to man or beast'. Not until the late 18th century did it became fashionable to admire wild and picturesque scenery.

When you reach the tip of Crummock Water you get a superb sense of the grandeur of the mountains that surround it. Coleridge loved the wildness of the Lakes and was never deterred by rain or bad weather. Unfortunately this worsened his rheumatism, a condition he tried to ease by drinking laudanum, known locally as 'Kendal Black Drop'. He was soon addicted to it.

Your route now takes you through Lanthwaite Woods and down the eastern side of the lake, where trees dip into the water like cats gently lapping at a bowl of cream. The scene can hardly have changed from Coleridge's time. An ancient bridlepath takes you away from the lake and over Rannerdale Knots, where thick carpets of bluebells wait to greet you in the spring. As you ramble back into Buttermere you begin to understand the spell cast by this hidden valley which helped to make the Lake District the Poets' Corner of England.

½ mile

½ km

H

7 Pass through a kissing gate and follow the shore, then take a gravel path through woods. At the far end cross a footbridge, then go through a kissing gate. Turn left up field to another kissing gate, then immediately turn right around foot of crag. On reaching a footbridge, cross it and turn left, signed Buttermere village, and follow riverside path back to car park.

705
▲
Gasgale Crags

Gasgale Gill

e
n

ite
arm

Brackenthwaite Fell

Grasmoor
▲
851

Herdwick sheep

Right: a kestrel hovers on the wind
Below: Claife Heights seen from
Latterbarrow. The narrow finger of
Windermere points to Ambleside

Claife Heights and a View of Windermere

The National Trust's estate at Claife, on the western shore of Windermere, is noted for the beauty of its setting and particularly for the rich diversity of habitats and landscapes to be found along its quiet winding paths. At the start of this walk the shoreline of the lake has the character of parkland in which nature's rougher edges have been trimmed and tamed. Beech trees overhang the water, swans bask on the close-cropped grass and even the woodland on the hills seems designed as a dramatic backdrop for gentle strolls and picnics. The grounds were laid out early in the 19th century by the Curwen family of Belle Isle, the curious circular mansion

2

Claife He
View of

The Victorians tried to 'im
moorland walk w

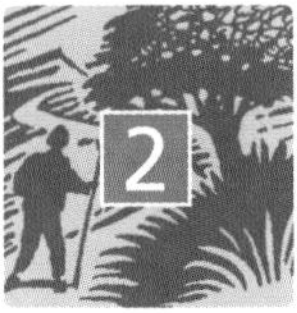

1 Turn left (north) out of car park and follow the lakeside for 2 miles (3.2km). The metalled lane soon becomes an unmade track through woodland.

2 As the track approaches Belle Grange turn left just before the house up a steep and stony bridleway, sign-posted to Letterbarrow and Near Sawrey. Ignoring a path to the left, continue on uphill (signposted to Hawkshead) until the path levels out and reaches a broad bridleway at a complex intersection.

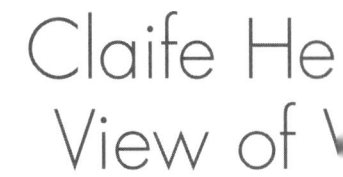

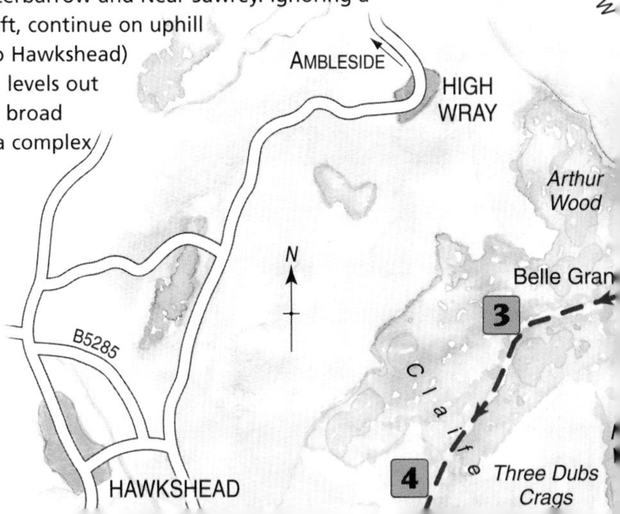
AMBLESIDE
HIGH WRAY
Arthur Wood
N
Belle Gran
3
B5285
Claife
4
Three Dubs Crags
HAWKSHEAD

Three
Dubs
Tarn

Wise
Een Tarn

Water
Side
Woods

Esthwaite
Water

Moss
Eccles Tarn

Cuckoo
Brow
Woods

Heights

5

NEAR
SAWREY

B5285

C
Sta

7

church

FAR
SAWREY

6

S
H

Claife Heights

Devil's
Gallop

Bishop Woods

3 Cross the bridle-
way and follow path
(signed to Sawrey via
Tarns) that bears slightly
to the left. Cross another intersection, still following the signs to
Sawrey, up a steep and stony path.
This soon joins a broader track that
passes through a gate and stile to reach
the open moorland on Claife Heights.

4 Follow faint path down towards the nearest
tarn, where the route becomes much clearer.
Follow trackway as it swings to left below an old
stone dam, passes through a wooden gate and dips
down to Moss Eccles Tarn. Continue on the track as
it drops down from the moor, splashes through a
little stream and runs between stone walls.

5 Wher
Sawrey b
bridlew
into Far S
st

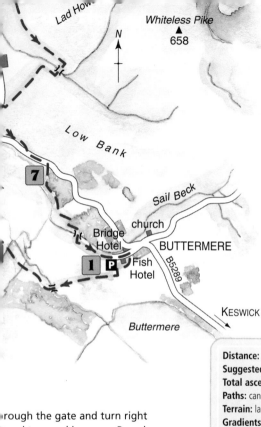

6 At the road walk left for a few paces then back up the bridleway leading uphill and over a shoulder. Follow the path, keeping the lake on your right. When it comes back to the road, continue to a group of pine trees.

Lad How

Whiteless Pike
▲
658

N

Low Bank

7

Sail Beck

church

Bridge Hotel **BUTTERMERE**

1 **P** Fish Hotel

B5289

KESWICK

Buttermere

rough the gate and turn right road to a parking area. Branch the hillside and soon cross the nd follow the bridleway. Go a gate, to a footbridge. Cross turn right to double-back and go down hill.

Distance: 7½ miles (12.1km)
Suggested map: OS Outdoor Leisure 4
Total ascent: 490ft (149m)
Paths: can be slippery and boggy
Terrain: lakeside tracks
Gradients: gradual
Refreshments: Kirkstile Inn, Loweswater; Fish Hotel and Bridge Hotel, Buttermere
Park: National Park car park near Bridge Hotel, Buttermere

an outcropping of igneous rocks in a way that will fascinate those with an interest in geology. The rocks have also yielded veins of copper ore and other minerals, notably at the Carrock End Mine, where the walk begins. Above Carrock End landscape becomes smooth and grassy. It is also largely featureless, and a confusing place in misty conditions. On a clear day, however, the top of High Pike – given its northerly position and the convenient memorial bench that stands

the crags at the eastern edge of the fell also contain outcrops of black gabbro, the rock of the Cuillins on Skye, and a rarity in Lakeland.

Carrock Fell is also unique in having a hill fort, of uncertain age, on its summit. Judging by the size of the collapsed walls that ring the summit, the fort must have been a large, important stronghold and a forbidding place to live.

Once you pass beyond Carrock Fell, the influence of Skiddaw slates takes over, and the

there – is one of the finest vantage points imaginable. To the south, the views are confined a little by the bulk of Blencathra and Skiddaw, but northwards the eye can scan the West Cumbrian Plain, the coastal flats of the Solway, and the hills of Dumfries and Galloway.

And when Lakeland throbs beneath the weight of summer and weekend visitors, it is among the fells 'Back o' Skidda' that peace and contentment will be found.

e – the
nd Hill

at a lonely viewpoint
olway Plain

Distance: 6 miles (9.7km)
Suggested map: OS Outdoor Leisure 5
Total ascent: 1,560ft (476m)
Paths: mostly clear, but not advised in
poor visibility; one short trackless
section
Terrain: mainly high mountain
moorland
Gradients: steep start but otherwise
moderate
Refreshments: Mill Inn at
Mungrisdale; pubs at Hesket Newmarket
and Caldbeck
Park: roadside parking on Caldbeck
Common, at site of Carrock End Mine,
1 mile north of Mosedale

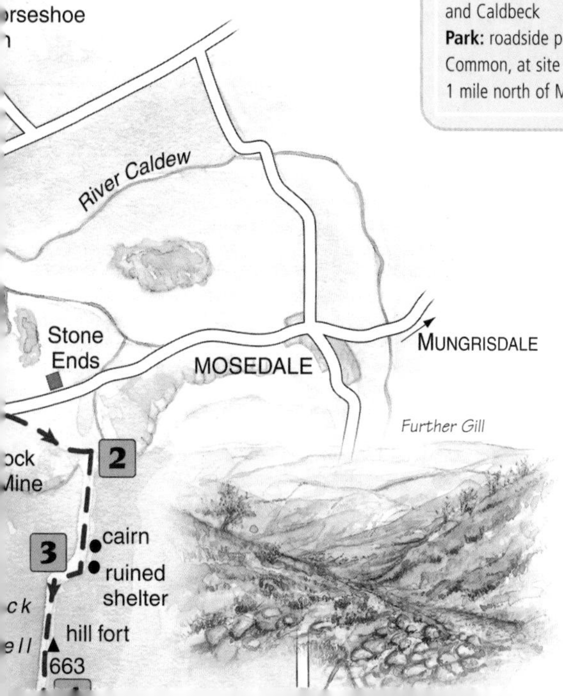

rseshoe

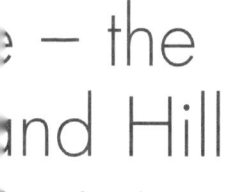

River Caldew

Stone
Ends   MOSEDALE

MUNGRISDALE

Further Gill

ock
Mine   **2**

3   • cairn
           • ruined
              shelter
c k
e l l   ▲ hill fort
         663

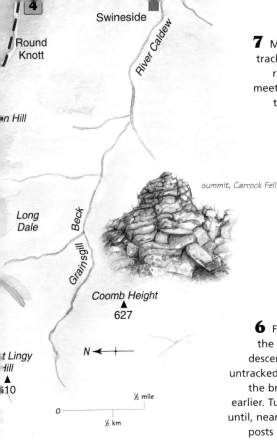

4

Round
Knott

Swineside

River Caldew

n Hill

Long
Dale

Beck

Grainsgill

summit, Carrock Fell

Coomb Height
▲
627

N ◄—+—

½ mile

0

½ km

t Lingy
Hill
▲
10

the path
of Drygill
d which it
summit, on
y track.

7 Much lower down the track forks again. Branch right and go down to meet the road. Turn right to return to the start.

6 From the summit face the distant Pennines and descend (eastwards) across untracked ground, to intersect the broad, stony track met earlier. Turn left, and follow it until, near three large wooden posts on the right, it forks. Branch right, until you reach the top of a narrow gully. Bear right again, alongside the gully and soon cross it to pursue an old mining track above Carrock Beck.

return to the Glassonby road and bear left up the hill out of the village. After ¼ mile (400m), opposite a signpost, turn left up an unsurfaced track that soon swings to the right and leads onto a metalled farm road. Continue straight ahead across a cattle grid to Long Meg stone circle.

2 From Long Meg, bear right off the farm road, following the footpath, signposted Glassonby, along the edge of two fields. Beyond a gate, continue with a stone wall to your left, then, through another gate to pass a small plantation on your right. The path now runs beside stone walls, through fields that can be very muddy, and crosses a farm lane to reach Addingham church.

electricity sub-station

Throstle Hall

Highland Drove PH

GREAT SALKELD

PENRITH

B6142

River Eden

LANGWATHBY

1

3 Follow the path aroun out onto a lane that ru road. Turn left, towards G left at the village green to signposted to Kirkoswald downhill for 1 mile (1.6 across a stream, with a la

Long Meg a

A spectacular stone circ
are linked by a wall

Distance: 6 miles (9.7km)
Suggested map: OS Outdoor Leisure 5
Total ascent: 230ft (70m)
Paths: mainly good, but some muddy sections
Terrain: fields, woodland and riverside
Gradients: slight; one short steep section
Refreshments: The Watermill, Little Salkeld
(Mon, Tue, Wed; seasonal)
Park: beside small village green in Little
Salkeld, 1½ miles (2.4km) north of
Langwathby and the A686 Penrith-Alston
road. Turn left off road to Glassonby at sharp
right bend

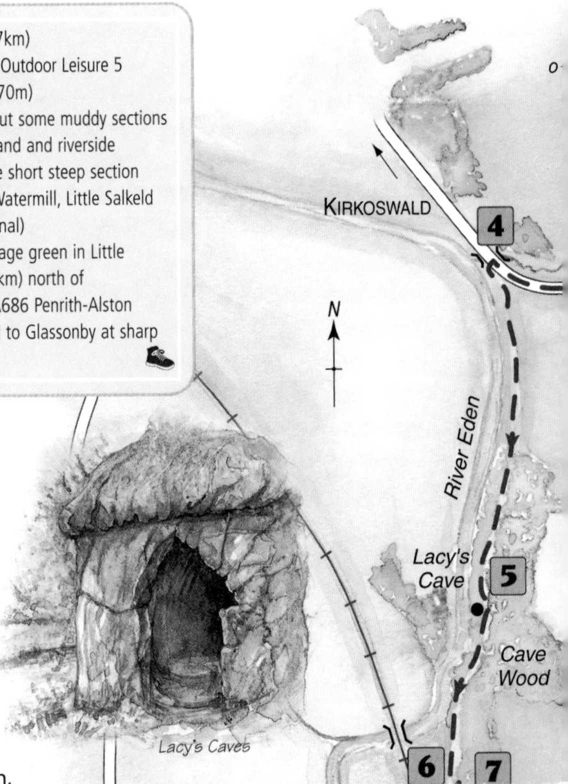

KIRKOSWALD

4

N

River Eden

Lacy's
Cave

5

Cave
Wood

Lacy's Caves

6 **7**

1 From the green,

Right: Long Meg, inscribed with cup and ring marks, stands apart from her daughters
Below: Colonel Lacy installed a live hermit to complete his caves

Long Meg and Lacy's Caves

Names, according to some old beliefs, are imbued with magic power, embodying the spirit of the person or the place they represent. Perhaps that is why the valley of the River Eden seems such a special place, harbouring more than its fair share of secrets.

As you leave Little Salkeld at the outset of this walk, the gentle landscape of the vale appears enclosed within an amphitheatre of high hills, with the Pennines to the east, Lakeland's mountains to the west and the Howgill Fells far off to the south. In prehistoric times this fertile, sheltered valley must have seemed a paradise compared with such wild uplands: a fitting site for one of northern England's most impressive neolithic monuments, and a place to sit and ponder ancient mysteries.

We can never know who built the shrine here, or why. The tall and slender monolith, known as Long Meg, with its huge ring of recumbent boulders – her 'daughters' – dates back at least 4,000 years and bears similarities to other monuments from Orkney to Stonehenge. Long Meg herself, etched with the distinctive circular and spiral patterns known as cup and ring marks, was dragged for well over a mile (1.6km) to the site. Count her daughters if you dare; according to legend, they are witches turned to stone for dancing on the Sabbath, and if you get their number right, they will come back to life.

Further on, in the porch of St Michael's Church, carved stones commemorate another mystery, the lost village of Addingham. For centuries local tales passed down

that can just be glimpsed through trees out on its private island.

The path climbs up into the hills behind Belle Grange where it runs through dense mixed woodland in which native broadleaves such as oak and ash are interspersed with larch plantations. So long as you are quiet, you may catch glimpses of red deer or notice a red squirrel darting up a tree. You may also see grey squirrels, which have advanced relatively recently into southern Lakeland and threaten to drive out the native red species.

As you emerge from the woodland on the summit of Claife Heights the views are unexpected and superb, of open moorland backed by distant prospects of the Furness Fells and Langdale Pikes. The tarns (upland ponds) that dot the moor are havens for wildfowl in any season of the year, and overhead you are likely to spot buzzards, or perhaps a kestrel hovering above the bracken. Although idyllic on a sunny day, the heights can be an eerie place on sombre autumn afternoons, when the roar of rutting stags might make you wonder if you've heard the legendary 'Claife Crier', a melancholy ghost that is said to haunt the area.

As the track descends it runs between old dry-stone walls enclosing fields of lush grass that have been cleared of stones, drained and fertilised by sheep (or, more recently, by chemical means). Despite its reputation as a wilderness, the Lake District is essentially a working landscape where nature has been made to serve the needs of humans.

There could scarcely be a better symbol of society's overly romantic view of nature than the bizarre castellated ruin of Claife Station. Built in 1799, when Windermere was first becoming a fashionable resort, the tower was a 'viewing station' with its windows carefully positioned to frame prospects of the lake and hills. Visitors would pay to see real landscapes framed to resemble paintings and on cloudy days they could, quite literally, view it through rose-tinted glass. Returning to the parkland on the shore you may ponder on the fact that nature always, ultimately, triumphs over art.

ts and the
ndermere

he beauty of this lake and
antic architecture

8 At far end of this car park, take footpath into woods and up
steps to Claife Station. At top of steps turn right along the terrace
walk, which drops down to the road. Turn left, then bear
immediately left along a narrow lane to return to car park.

7 Turn left down the hill,
then cross the road onto
footpath separated from
the traffic by a wall.
Follow path downhill
and across the road,
through woodland
to a car park.

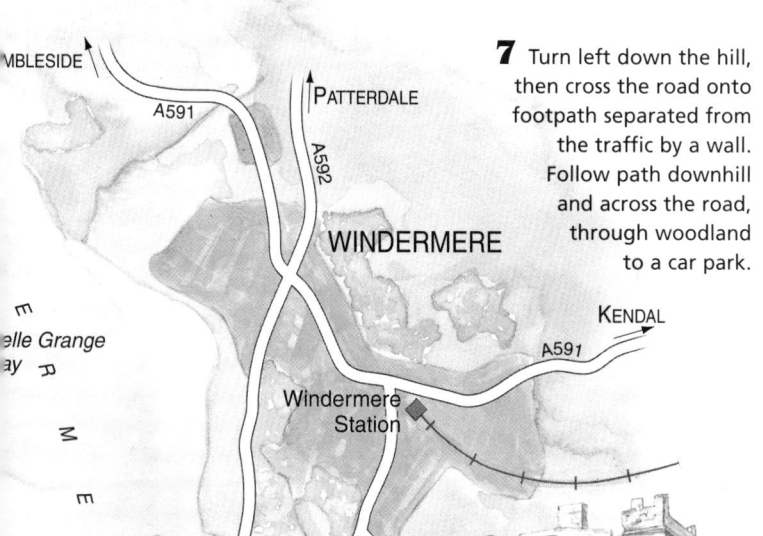

MBLESIDE

A591

PATTERDALE

A592

WINDERMERE

KENDAL

A591

elle Grange
ay

Windermere
Station

m

Belle Isle

BOWNESS-ON-WINDERMERE

Claife Station

B5284 KENDAL

ferry

A5074

A592

SEDGWICK

6 Just beyond the hotel car park bear left up a track signposted to ferry. The footpath skirts the gardens of a private house, then drops towards the lake beside a high stone wall. Continue on across a driveway, down a path through overhanging rhododendrons, to the road.

½ mile

0

½ km

NEWBY BRIDGE

forks to Near and Far
ough a gate and follow
join a metalled lane
left along the village
Sawrey Hotel.

Distance: 8 miles (12.9km)
Suggested map: OS Outdoor Leisure 7
Total ascent: 495ft (151m)
Paths: mainly good, but some rough and boggy sections
Terrain: woodland, open moorland, farmland
Gradients: some steep sections
Refreshments: Sawrey Hotel
Park: Harrow Slack National Trust car park, off the B5285 on the west shore of Windermere, 200yds (182m) along the lakeside lane northwest of Bowness Ferry

Great How
▲
518

Crag
▲
444
High Scarth
Crag

Beck

Cowcove

Scale Gill

Stony
Tarn

waterfall
Scale Bridge

River

7

3 Cross the bridge and climb left, still alongside, but well above, the river. Two pronounced rises follow before the path reaches Scar Lathing, where the river makes a distinct bend westwards. Cross an inflowing stream, and bear left to pass beneath Scar Lathing, beyond which lies the bleak arena of Great Moss, spread below the soaring heights of Sca Fell and the lower cliffs of Cam Spout Crag.

Taw House
Farm

Har

Brotherilk
Farm

Birdhow

RAVENGLASS
BOOT

1

P

0

½ km

4 The moss is invariably waterlogged and paths sketchy, but the objective is now to cross the river. This is usually best accomplished at or just above the confluence with How Beck, and is rarely completed dryshod. Once across, head towards the base of the waterfall from How Beck, then turn left and contour along the base of a rocky slope to reach a small knoll with massive boulders, known as Sampson's Stones.

5 A sho
reached. Fr
climb away
landscape

The Contrasts

From a lowland vale to
following the River Esk ir

1 Begin from a roadside parking area at the foot
of Hardknott Pass, and descend to follow the
access to Brotherilkeld Farm (right, by the tele-
phone box). As you near the farm, branch left
on a path parallel with the River Esk. Ignore
a footbridge and continue up-river.

2 Beyond a gate
follow a broad track
crossing rough
pasture. This leads
past a series of
delightful water-
falls, and ultimately
arrives at Lingcove
Bridge, directly
below the crags of
Throstle Garth.

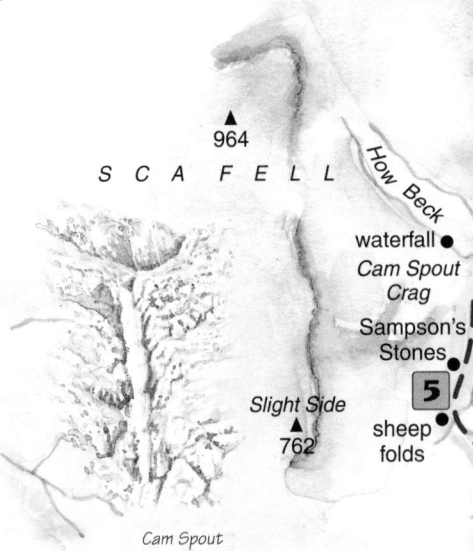

Scafell Pike
▲
978

▲
964

S C A F E L L

How Beck

waterfall ●
*Cam Spout
Crag*

Sampson's
Stones

5

Slight Side
▲
762

sheep
folds

Cam Spout

Silverybie

Right: looking towards Bowfell from remote Upper Eskdale
Below: yellow flowers of roseroot cling to the damp crags

The Contrasts of Upper Eskdale

In few places do the rivers of Lakeland truly rival those of the Scottish glens, but the River Esk, draining the vast upland sponge of Great Moss and gathering the waters of England's highest peaks, most certainly does. Between its confluences with Scale Gill and Lingcove Beck, the river puts on a fine show of white water, crashing over rock steps and diving headlong into crystal plunge pools. Above, the cliffs of Hard Knott and Heron Crags are as dark as the ravens they host, and a perfect framework for the Esk and the countless gills that feed it.

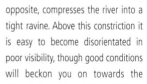

At Lingcove Bridge the setting is impressive: steep fells rise on either hand, while the way forward is split by the rocky upthrust of Throstle Garth. The sound of water is constant, echoing off the rock walls and adding drama to an already outstanding landscape. Mist adds a new dimension, wreathing the crags and signalling to the less experienced walker to proceed with caution and to retreat when route certainty ebbs towards doubt.

Beyond the bridge two distinct ascents follow; the second across the shoulder of Throstlehow Crag, which, with Green Crag opposite, compresses the river into a tight ravine. Above this constriction it is easy to become disorientated in poor visibility, though good conditions will beckon you on towards the craggy heights of Sca Fell and its neighbour, Scafell Pike, the highest summit in England.

Great Moss invokes delight or despair according to one's view of things bleak and barren. It is a vast water-gathering sponge of grass and reeds that captures rainfall from a massive ring of summits. Here the indistinct remains of a turf wall mark the boundary of a deer enclosure constructed long ago by the monks of Furness Abbey; now all this is National Trust property.

Sca Fell and Scafell Pike dominate the scene, but it is Great Moss that is the objective of this walk. Here, amid the empty vastness, the sense of isolation and loneliness is heightened by the absence of features. Bogs and deep streams await the unwary, and somehow the only certainty seems to be that you are going to get wet. So convincing is this feeling that most walkers simply choose the shallowest part of the river to cross, and surrender themselves to a foot-soaking paddle.

But the air of wilderness is overwhelmingly powerful, the ramparts of soaring pinnacles and buttresses dramatic, and the emptiness awe-inspiring. Here is the heart of Lakeland, littered with debris from the crags above, a spectacle of nature's strength, and a humbling, magnificent place to be.

Upper Eskdale

d's highest mountains,
emote heart of Lakeland

7 A short way beyond the bridge, take the lower of two ladder stiles, and follow an improving track to Taw House Farm. Immediately turn left over a ladder stile and go down an enclosed path to the footbridge across the Esk encountered at the start of the walk, and from there retrace your steps to the valley road.

6 The path, passing below Silverybield Crag, Round Scar and Rowantree Crags, is clear throughout, but occasionally resorts to evasion tactics before breaking free of the rocks on reaching Scale Gill. Now a clear green path zigzags down through bracken, turns right at the bottom and crosses Scale Bridge, where the gill puts on an impressive show of force.

Yeastyrigg
Crags

er Esk

eat
oss

Long Crag
▲
492

car
thing

Birker Fell

Lingcove Beck

Throstlehow
Crag

Throstle

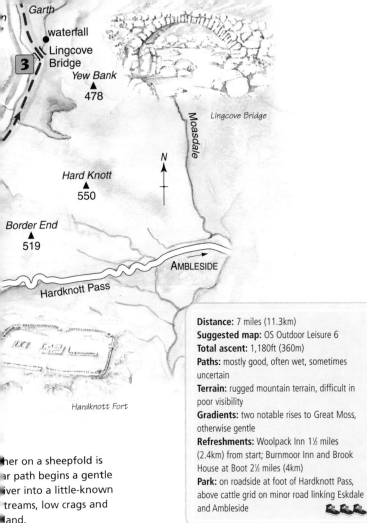

Garth

waterfall

Lingcove
3 Bridge

Yew Bank
▲ 478

Moasdale

Lingcove Bridge

↑ N

Hard Knott
▲ 550

Border End
▲ 519

AMBLESIDE →

Hardknott Pass

Hardknott Fort

ner on a sheepfold is
ar path begins a gentle
iver into a little-known
treams, low crags and
and.

Distance: 7 miles (11.3km)
Suggested map: OS Outdoor Leisure 6
Total ascent: 1,180ft (360m)
Paths: mostly good, often wet, sometimes
uncertain
Terrain: rugged mountain terrain, difficult in
poor visibility
Gradients: two notable rises to Great Moss,
otherwise gentle
Refreshments: Woolpack Inn 1½ miles
(2.4km) from start; Burnmoor Inn and Brook
House at Boot 2½ miles (4km)
Park: on roadside at foot of Hardknott Pass,
above cattle grid on minor road linking Eskdale
and Ambleside

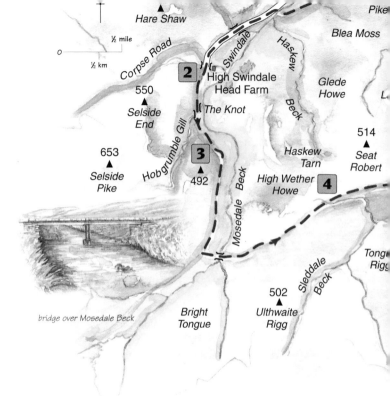

Hare Shaw

Pike

Blea Moss

½ mile

0

½ km

Corpse Road

Swindale

Haskew

2 High Swindale Head Farm

Glede Howe

550

The Knot

Selside End

Hobgrumble Gill

Beck

653 ▲ Selside Pike

3 ▲ 492

Haskew Tarn

514 ▲ Seat Robert

High Wether Howe **4**

Mosedale Beck

bridge over Mosedale Beck

Sleddale Beck

Tongue Rigg

Bright Tongue

502 ▲ Ulthwaite Rigg

3 Keep on until a bridge spanning Mosedale Beck comes into view. Stay on the path to a vehicle track cutting down to the bridge. On the other side ascend one of the tracks which climb onto a broad grassy ridge, rising to a fence and gate. Beyond, a grassy track climbs further. When this forks, branch right.

4 After a s into Wet Sle stile leave the zags to Sle lower track, th forward to follow a roug

Swindale and

Exploring forgotten valleys

1 Leave Keld on a moorland road to Tailbert Farm. At Tailbert, abandon the road for a track across the hillside, later descending through bracken and gorse into Swindale. Cross a ford or a nearby bridge. Turn left, follow the minor road to Swindale Head Farm and go through gates onto a bridleway signed Mosedale.

2 After a final building on the left, branch left through glacial moraine, and climb through the rocky outcrops of Selside Pike. Cross open moorland to a fence at Swine Gill. Go through a gate and continue to a dilapidated building and a collapsed wall nearby.

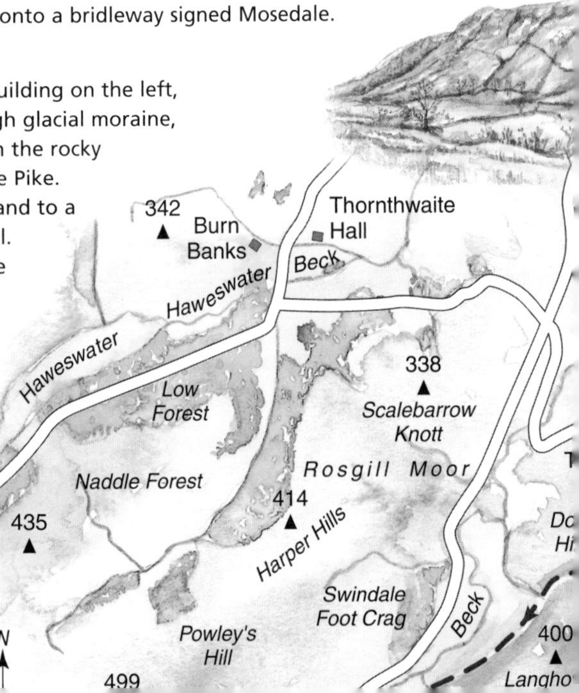

342 ▲ Burn Banks

Thornthwaite Hall

Beck

Haweswater Beck

Haweswater

Haweswater

Low Forest

338 ▲ Scalebarrow Knott

Naddle Forest

Rosgill Moor

414 ▲

Harper Hills

435 ▲

Swindale Foot Crag

Beck

Do Hi

400

Langho

N

Powley's Hill

499

4

Right *peregrine falcons haunt the crags*
above lonely Swindale
Below: *Herdwick and Swaledale sheep graze*
the flanks of Dog Hill

Swindale and the Eastern Fells

Isolated Swindale – 'the valley of the swine' – offers a vivid picture of a glacier-fashioned landscape that can have changed little since the first farmers arrived some 6,000 years ago. As you cross the gorsey flanks of Dog Hill, the valley eases into view below, curving progressively southward to an abrupt end, where an old road used for transporting corpses from Mardale (now under Haweswater reservoir) enters the valley en route for Shap.

Above the dale head, Mosedale Beck flows through a shallow, V-shaped moorland valley before plummeting into the waterfalls of Swindale Forces. Nearby Hobgrumble Gill fills a dark gash in the cliff face with waters seeping from a high corrie on Selside Pike. When the two streams combine amid glacial moraine they produce Swindale Beck, a rare highlight in a sombre, craggy dale. Mosedale and Hobgrumble

corrie are both hanging valleys, cut off by the weight of ice that ground away at the sediments and rocks of the main valley floor, lowering it appreciably.

Other than on foot, horseback or a bicycle, there is no way through Swindale, and no immediately apparent through passage for anyone. The sense of remoteness is great on the long descent into the dale. Here, after the Romans had retreated, the Vikings came. Ancient records note the local name 'Thengeheved' – 'the council place at the head of the valley'.

Now the cliffs, shelter peregrines, buzzards and visiting golden eagles, while the short days of winter see flocks of travel-weary fieldfares, mistle thrushes, redwings and a scattering of bramblings feeding in the fields and whirling across the cliff faces.

Above Swindale Head and the ruins of High Swindale Head Farm, Mosedale offers only the emptiness of grassy moorland across which red deer roam freely, and where, in autumn, the sound of a stag at the rut echoes sharply. Mosedale is untamed and empty, save for a collapsed wall and a small sheepfold, a flowing expanse of tough sheep's fescue and common bent. The way across it begins hesitantly and continues uncertainly, and the feeling of isolation is heightened by the barren scenery.

The distant Mosedale Cottage, surrounded by its stand of trees, lies mid-way between Swindale and Long Sleddale, and is a forlorn spot below the spoil of the disused Mosedale Quarry. Leaving this empty quarter the walk climbs into Wet Sleddale. Here, in spring, flocks of black-headed gulls wheel and launch into sudden 'dreads' as they all take screaming to the air. In the far distance, the high northern Pennines fringe the skyline, while near by the dark waters of the reservoir reflect the sky's moods in an endlessly changing display.

6 When the river makes a pronounced bend to the right, move away from it to a wall. Go past Steps Hall, following a rough track towards Thornship Farm. Opposite the farm continue alongside the river to reach Keld once more.

5 Follow the road to a cattle grid. Here leave the road, turning left alongside the River Lowther. Cross a road and continue beside the river.

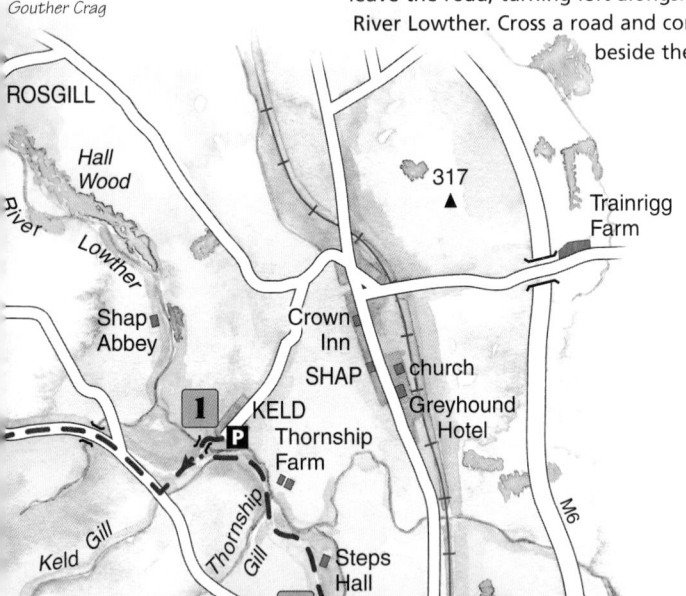

Gouther Crag

ROSGILL

Hall Wood

River Lowther

▲ 317

Trainrigg Farm

Shap Abbey

Crown Inn

SHAP

church

Greyhound Hotel

1 KELD

Thornship Farm

Keld Gill

Thornship Gill

Steps Hall

M6

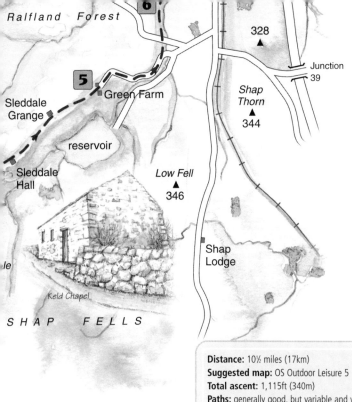

Ralfland Forest

6

328 ▲

Junction 39

5

Green Farm

Sleddale Grange

Shap Thorn 344 ▲

reservoir

Low Fell 346 ▲

Sleddale Hall

le

Shap Lodge

Keld Chapel

SHAP FELLS

the path descends
the second ladder
and turn down zig-
Here go down to a
te beside a barn and
ange. Beyond this
road to Green Farm.

Distance: 10½ miles (17km)
Suggested map: OS Outdoor Leisure 5
Total ascent: 1,115ft (340m)
Paths: generally good, but variable and wet in Mosedale
Terrain: moorland and cultivated valleys
Gradients: mostly gentle; one steep ascent
Refreshment: Shap; Keld (seasonal)
Park: Keld, on minor road west of A6 at Shap

section, and follow a green path through heather and bracken, passing a small cairn and a ruined shelter.

3 The path rises easily to the east peak of Carrock Fell, from where a broad track strikes westwards to the main summit. On the way you pass through a ring of stones that once formed a substantial hill fort. A large cairn on a rocky plinth crowns the summit, with a shelter nearby.

4 From just north of the summit a path heads westwards across a broad ridge, passing to the north of Round Knott before reaching grassy Miton Hill. From here, walk northwest on a broad grassy track, passing Red Gate, an obvious cross-track, which offers a quick escape route northwards if necessary.

7

Carrock Bec

West Fell

● Driggith Mine

Drygill

CALDBECK
FELLS

6 ● large cairn

657
High Pike

summit, High Pike

5 As you approach curves northwards to Beck, a steep-sided ra ascends easy grassy slo the way crossing a

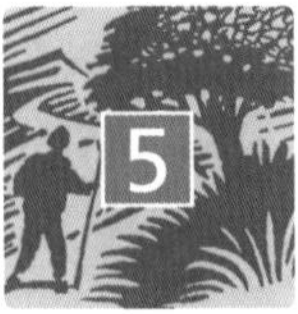

1 From the site of the old Carrock End Mine on Caldbeck Common head for a conspicuous grassy path slanting left and up across the lower slopes of Carrock Fell. The path climbs steeply to meet Further Gill Sike.

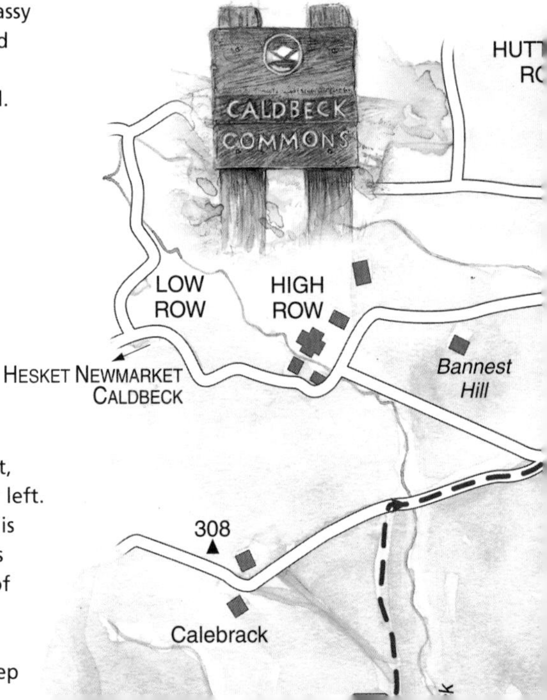

CALDBECK COMMONS

HUT
RC

LOW ROW

HIGH ROW

Bannest Hill

HESKET NEWMARKET
CALDBECK

2 Here branch right, with the gill on your left. Higher up, the gully is dry and the path less distinct. At the top of the gully, climb straight on through heather to a less steep

308 ▲

Calebrack

High Pike – the Last Lakeland Hill

Behind the formidable barrier of Blencathra and Skiddaw lie the delectable Caldbeck and Uldale fells, a region of peace and isolation where rounded, grassy hills offer easy exploration, free from constraining walls and fences. Carrock Fell is the only exception, and betrays a significant change in the underlying rock strata.

This is a corner of heaven set aside for lovers of solitude, a wild and intriguing place, unique in Lakeland. Now virtually treeless and completely uncultivated, these infrequently visited northern fells were a true forest in olden times, and more recently a forest in the sense of a hunting reserve. They were also the hunting ground of John Peel, immortalised in the verses

of 'D'ye ken John Peel'. Born in nearby Caldbeck in 1776, one of 13 children, Peel himself fathered 13 children. He and his bride, the daughter of a wealthy farmer from Uldale and then only 18 years old, were wed at Gretna Green after her mother had objected to the union. Begrudgingly, the family accepted that the two were indeed married, but insisted on a service of re-marriage at Caldbeck church. It was about this time that Peel started hunting with his own pack of hounds, and often followed them on foot, in the traditional Lakeland manner.

Of the two principal summits visited on this walk, Carrock Fell has the greater interest. To begin with, the Skiddaw slates that underlie the rest of the northern fells here terminate against